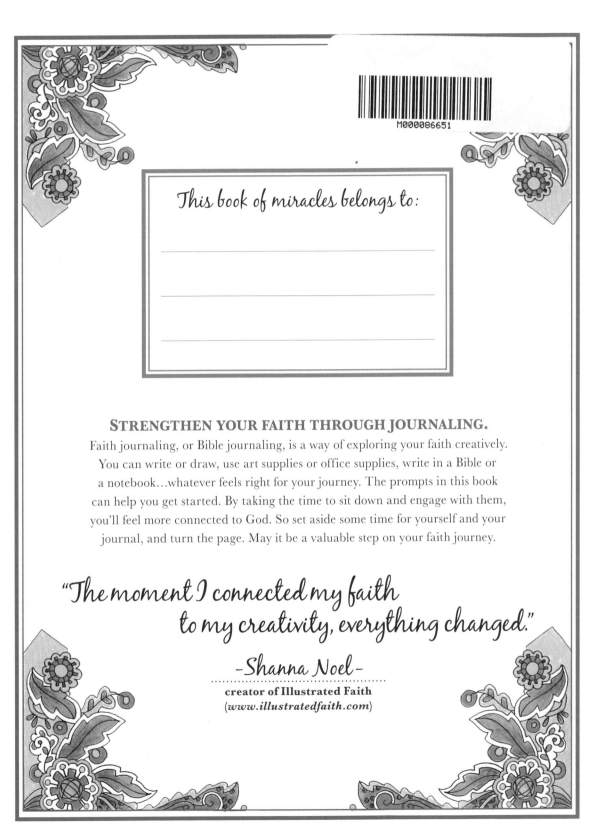

This book of miracles belongs to:

_____

_____

_____

STRENGTHEN YOUR FAITH THROUGH JOURNALING.

Faith journaling, or Bible journaling, is a way of exploring your faith creatively. You can write or draw, use art supplies or office supplies, write in a Bible or a notebook…whatever feels right for your journey. The prompts in this book can help you get started. By taking the time to sit down and engage with them, you'll feel more connected to God. So set aside some time for yourself and your journal, and turn the page. May it be a valuable step on your faith journey.

"The moment I connected my faith to my creativity, everything changed."

–Shanna Noel–

creator of Illustrated Faith
(*www.illustratedfaith.com*)

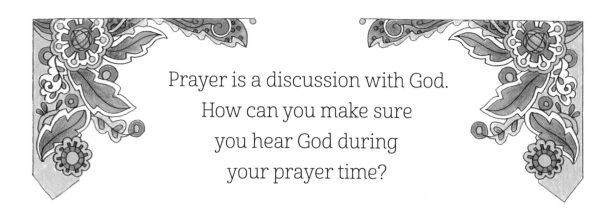

Prayer is a discussion with God.
How can you make sure
you hear God during
your prayer time?

Rise up &
PRAY

Luke 22:46

How can you and God
work together
to improve you?

_____
_____
_____
_____
_____
_____
_____
_____
_____
_____
_____
_____
_____
_____
_____
_____
_____
_____

I am the
vine,
you are the
branches.
If you remain in me
and I in you,
you will bear
much
fruit.

John 15:5

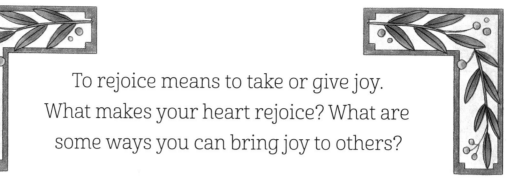

To rejoice means to take or give joy.
What makes your heart rejoice? What are
some ways you can bring joy to others?

Rejoice *in the* Lord

Philippians 4:4

What makes
a house a home?

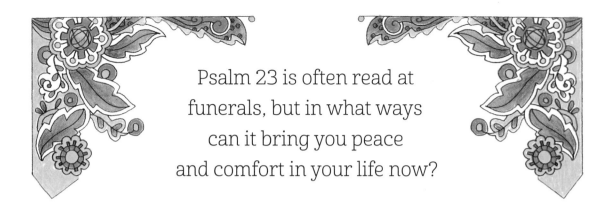

Psalm 23 is often read at
funerals, but in what ways
can it bring you peace
and comfort in your life now?

My cup overflows with your *blessings*

PSALM 23:5

What are some ways you can allow God to be your protector and refuge?

_____
_____
_____
_____
_____
_____
_____
_____
_____
_____
_____
_____
_____
_____
_____
_____
_____

He will cover you with his *feathers* and under his WINGS you will find *Refuge*

PSALM 91:4

As a society, we tend to say
"thank you" frequently,
but what does it mean to be
truly grateful?

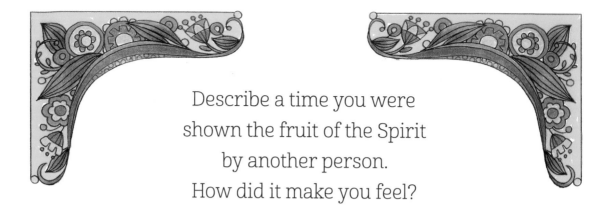

Describe a time you were
shown the fruit of the Spirit
by another person.
How did it make you feel?

_____

_____

_____

_____

_____

_____

_____

_____

_____

_____

_____

_____

_____

_____

_____

_____

_____

the Fruit of the Spirit is love, joy, peace, patience, kindness, goodness, faithfulness, gentleness, and self-control.

Galatians 5:22-23

Is forgiveness an act
that you do for yourself
or for others? Why?

Does this verse bring you
peace or cause you anxiety?
Why?

IN HIS *Heart* A MAN PLANS HIS *Course* BUT THE *Lord* DETERMINES HIS *Steps*

PROVERBS 16:9

21

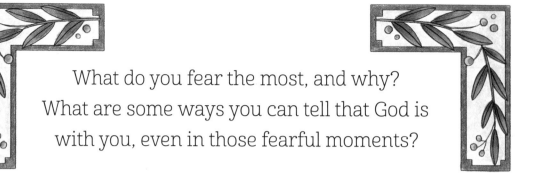

What do you fear the most, and why?
What are some ways you can tell that God is
with you, even in those fearful moments?

_____
_____
_____
_____
_____
_____
_____
_____
_____
_____
_____
_____
_____
_____
_____
_____
_____

Fear not, for I am with you.

Isaiah 41:10

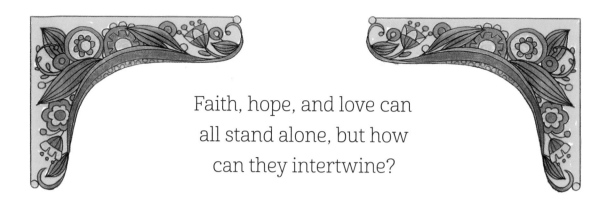

Faith, hope, and love can
all stand alone, but how
can they intertwine?

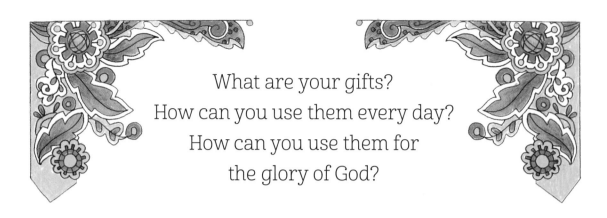

What are your gifts?
How can you use them every day?
How can you use them for
the glory of God?

every good and Perfect Gift is from above ——James 1:17

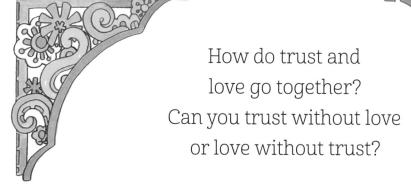

How do trust and
love go together?
Can you trust without love
or love without trust?

tRUSt
without wavering

PSALM 26:1

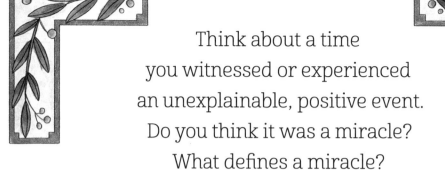

Think about a time
you witnessed or experienced
an unexplainable, positive event.
Do you think it was a miracle?
What defines a miracle?

NOTHING WILL BE IMPOSSIBLE WITH GOD

LUKE 1:37

How might the world change
if everything were
done in love?

LET ALL THAT YOU DO BE DONE IN LOVE – 1 CORINTHIANS 16:14

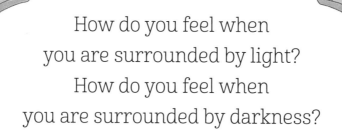

How do you feel when
you are surrounded by light?
How do you feel when
you are surrounded by darkness?

I am the LIGHT of the world

John 8:12

How can you
develop or nurture
a gentle, loving heart?

gentle loving heart, full of Peace

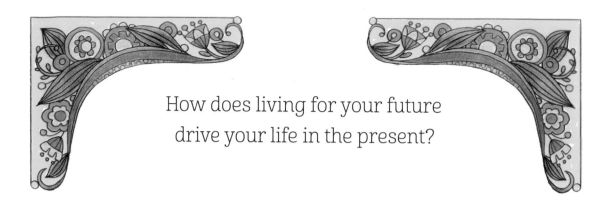

How does living for your future
drive your life in the present?

"For I know the plans I have for you",
says the Lord."They are plans for good
and not for evil, to give you a
future and a hope".

Jeremiah 29:11

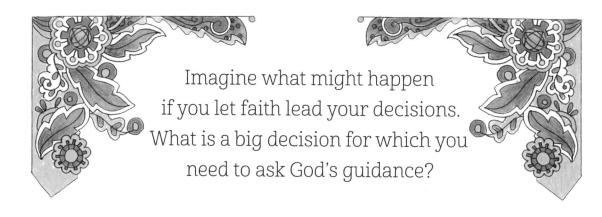

Imagine what might happen
if you let faith lead your decisions.
What is a big decision for which you
need to ask God's guidance?

Faith guides me

How can you
develop or nurture
a gentle, loving heart?

...and the greatest of these is Love

1 CORINTHIANS 13:13

Nature allows us to see
and experience God's presence.
Describe a time you felt
God's presence in nature.

You, Oh God, make the dawn and the sunset shout for joy.

Psalm 65:8b

What does it mean
to cling to what is good?
List some things that
are good in your life.

Cling to that which is good

ROMANS 12:9

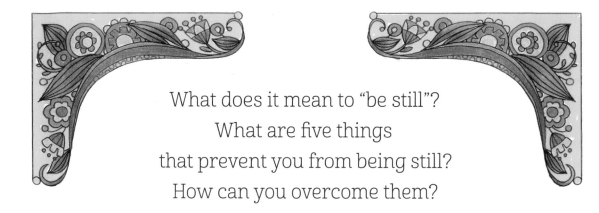

What does it mean to "be still"?
What are five things
that prevent you from being still?
How can you overcome them?

Be Still and know that I am GOD

PSALM 46:10

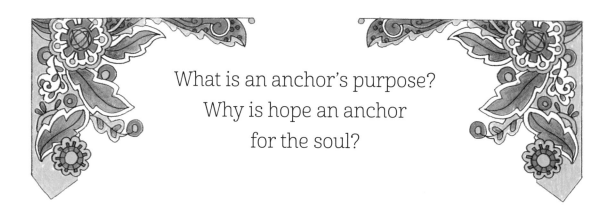

What is an anchor's purpose?
Why is hope an anchor
for the soul?

THIS HOPE WE HAVE AS AN ANCHOR OF THE SOUL, A HOPE BOTH SURE AND STEADFAST

Hebrews 6:19

List five ways you are blessed.
Then list five ways
you can bless others.

What do
answers to prayer
depend on?

_____

_____

_____

_____

_____

_____

_____

_____

_____

_____

_____

_____

_____

_____

_____

_____

_____

_____

_____

Therefore I tell you, whatever you ask for in prayer, believe that you have received it and it will be yours

Mark 11:24

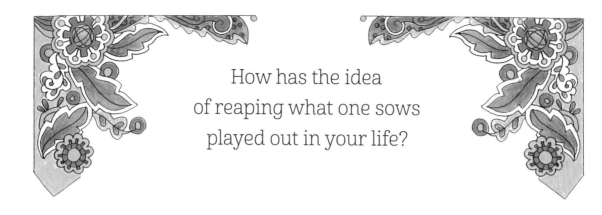

How has the idea
of reaping what one sows
played out in your life?

whatever
one sows,

GALATIANS 6:7

that will he also Reap

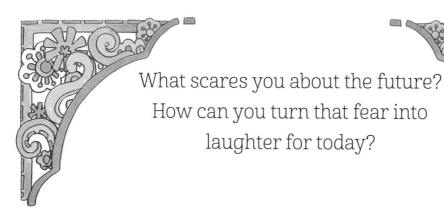

What scares you about the future?
How can you turn that fear into
laughter for today?

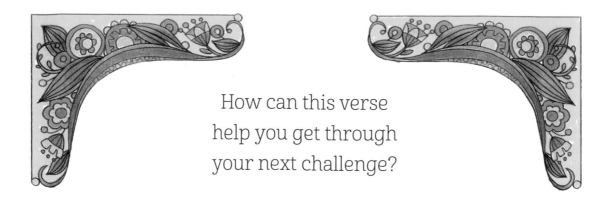

How can this verse
help you get through
your next challenge?

GOD is Within HER She Will Not fall

Psalm 46:5

Think of some ways
you can facilitate harmony
in your workplace or home.

Live in harmony with one another, be sympathetic, live as brothers, be compassionate and humble.

1 Peter 3:8

What are your treasures?
Where is your heart?

For where your
Treasure is,

family

there will your
heart be also

Luke 12:34

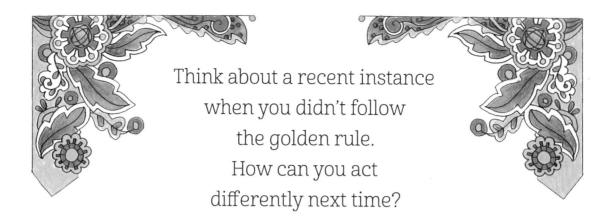

Think about a recent instance
when you didn't follow
the golden rule.
How can you act
differently next time?

Do unto others as you would have them do unto you.

Matthew 7:12

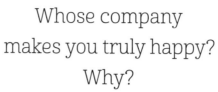
Whose company
makes you truly happy?
Why?

YOU LEAD ME IN THE *path of life;*

I EXPERIENCE ABSOLUTE *joy in your presence;*

YOU ALWAYS GIVE ME *sheer delight.*

PSALM 16:11

What does strength
look like to you?

"...THOSE WHO KEEP WAITING
FOR THE LORD
WILL RENEW THEIR STRENGTH.
THEN THEY'LL SOAR ON
WINGS LIKE EAGLES..."

ISAIAH 40:31

How does your family
give you strength?

_____
_____
_____
_____
_____
_____
_____
_____
_____
_____
_____
_____
_____
_____
_____
_____
_____

find Strength in
faith &
family

What are some things
you need to ask
for God's help with?

I lift up my eyes to
the mountains—
where does my help come from?
My help comes from the Lord,
the Maker of heaven and earth.

Psalm 121:1-2

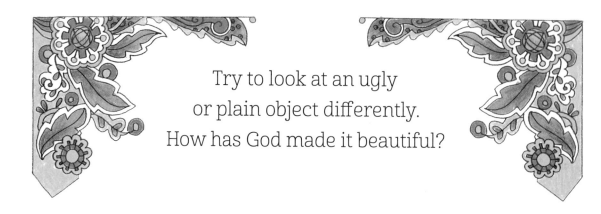

Try to look at an ugly
or plain object differently.
How has God made it beautiful?

What is the difference
between being smart
and having wisdom?

_____
_____
_____
_____
_____
_____
_____
_____
_____
_____
_____
_____
_____
_____
_____
_____
_____
_____
_____

WISDOM

is a tree of life
to those who embrace
her; happy are those
who hold her tightly.

PROVERBS 3:18

What is the difference between
joy and happiness?

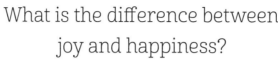

the joy of the LORD is your strength

Nehemiah 8:10

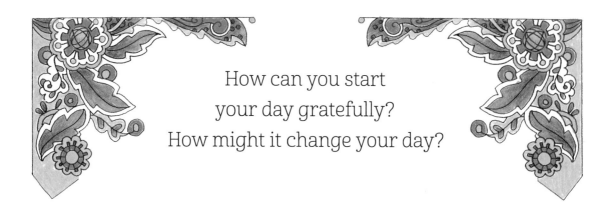

How can you start
your day gratefully?
How might it change your day?

start each day with a grateful heart

Why should we gather
before giving thanks?

What is a concrete way
that you can walk in faith
rather than sight?

_____

_____

_____

_____

_____

_____

_____

_____

_____

_____

_____

_____

_____

_____

_____

_____

for we walk by faith, not by sight.

2 Corinthians 5:7

What are you
most afraid of?
How can you move
past that fear?

don't be afraid, just believe

Mark 5:36

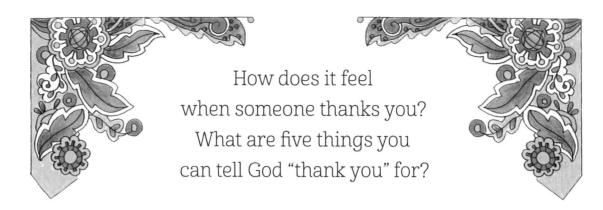

How does it feel
when someone thanks you?
What are five things you
can tell God "thank you" for?

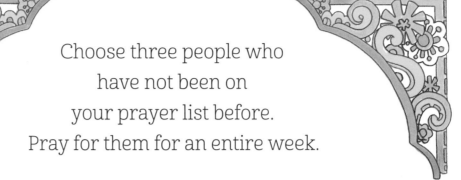

Choose three people who
have not been on
your prayer list before.
Pray for them for an entire week.

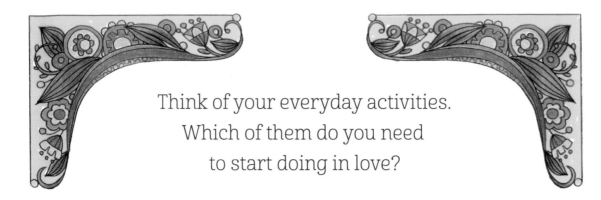

Think of your everyday activities.
Which of them do you need
to start doing in love?

Let all that you do be done in LOVE

1 Corinthians 16:14

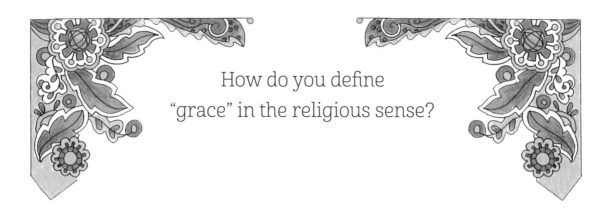

How do you define
"grace" in the religious sense?

Think of someone in your life
who needs your forgiveness.
How can you begin
to forgive them?

be forgiving and compassionate

List some concrete ways
that you personally
can serve God.

AS FOR ME AND MY HOUSE, WE WILL SERVE the LORD.

JOSHUA 24:15

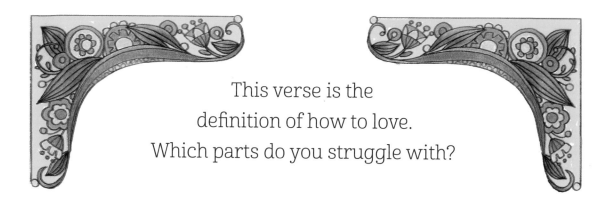

This verse is the
definition of how to love.
Which parts do you struggle with?

_____

_____

_____

_____

_____

_____

_____

_____

_____

_____

_____

_____

_____

_____

_____

_____

_____

_____

_____

_____

Love is patient
and kind;
love does not envy
or boast;
it is not arrogant
or rude.
It does not insist
on its own way;
it is not irritable
or resentful;
it does not rejoice
at wrongdoing,
but rejoices with
the truth.
Love bears all things,
believes all things,
hopes all things,
endures all things.

1 Corinthians 13:4-7

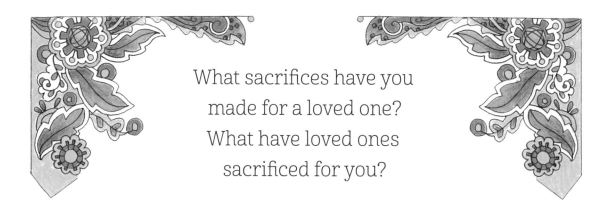

What sacrifices have you
made for a loved one?
What have loved ones
sacrificed for you?

For God so loved the world...

John 3:16

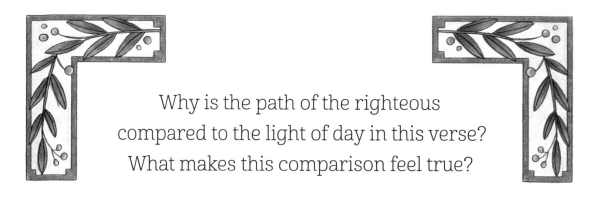

Why is the path of the righteous compared to the light of day in this verse? What makes this comparison feel true?

THE PATH OF THE RIGHTEOUS IS LIKE THE MORNING SUN.
SHINING EVER BRIGHTER LIKE THE FULL LIGHT OF DAY.

PROVERBS 4:18

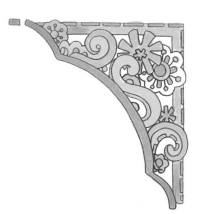

Reflect on a time
in your life
when you witnessed
God taking control.

with God all things are possible.

MATTHEW 19:26

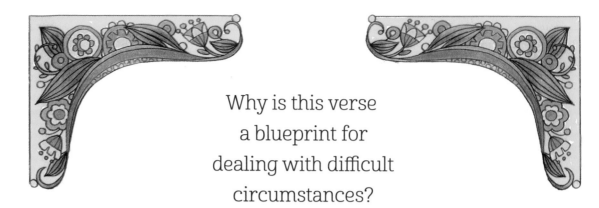

Why is this verse
a blueprint for
dealing with difficult
circumstances?

Be
JOYFUL
in hope,
PATIENT
in affliction,
FAITHFUL
in prayer.

ROMANS 12:12

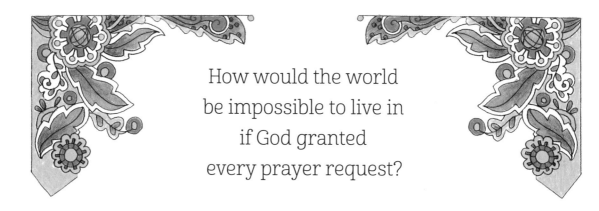

How would the world
be impossible to live in
if God granted
every prayer request?

FOR EVERYONE WHO ASKS RECEIVES.

AND THE ONE WHO SEEKS FINDS.

AND TO THE ONE WHO KNOCKS. THE DOOR WILL BE OPENED.

MATTHEW 7:8

How does worship
alongside others
enrich your experience
with God?

For where two or three gather in my name, there I am with them.

Matthew 18:20

How would your attitude
change toward others
if you only looked at the good?

whatever is
TRUE
whatever is
NOBLE
whatever is
RIGHT
whatever is
PURE
whatever is
LOVELY
whatever is
ADMIRABLE
- if anything is
EXCELLENT
or
PRAISEWORTHY
- think about
such things

PHILIPPIANS 4:8

Glory to God

GOD IS LOVE

1 JOHN 4:16

_____
_____
_____
_____
_____
_____
_____
_____
_____
_____
_____
_____
_____
_____
_____
_____
_____
_____
_____
_____
_____
_____
_____
_____
_____
_____
_____
_____

ABOUT THE ARTIST

Robin Pickens grew up in a creative family, making drawing and art a natural choice for her. After earning her BFA from the University of Michigan School of Art, Robin worked for many years as a successful broadcast television art director and animator. She then chose to pursue her passion for creating art that speaks from her heart and reflects her creative life as a wife and mother. Robin licenses her artwork for a variety of products, including Christmas ornaments, fabrics, calendars, greeting cards, gift books, home décor, wall art, dishware, and more. You can find more of Robin's work at *www.spoonflower.com/profiles/robinpickens* as well as through her website, *www.robinpickens.com*.

ISBN 978-1-64178-002-5

Fox Chapel Publishing makes every effort to use environmentally friendly paper for printing.

© 2018 by Robin Pickens and Quiet Fox Designs; *www.QuietFoxDesigns.com*, an imprint of Fox Chapel Publishing, 800-457-9112, 903 Square Street, Mount Joy, PA 17552.

We are always looking for talented authors. To submit an idea, please send a brief inquiry to acquisitions@foxchapelpublishing.com.

Printed in China
First printing